Coronach

By

Craig Stobo

PublishNation
www.publishnation.co.uk

Acknowledgements

My thanks to everyone who read and commented on these poems: Lisa, Vetters, Begg, Scotchers, Wendy J, Cath Maw, Katie G, Leigh, Brodie, The Wilson, Carolyn, Eva, Morgan and Lucy. A version of Epicentre was published in Gutter 15.

In memoriam
Fiona Elizabeth Agnew
1974-2012
Isla Elspeth Elizabeth Stobo
Born asleep 25 August 2012

I followed your footsteps
until the tide
washed them all away;

now I am stranded,
surrounded by a col,
waiting for unseen dragons;

the sea sings to me,
but it is the music of others,
and I am deaf to it.

Contents

Unseen love poem

I wish for you
the mares' tails of the sky to guide you,
the silence of late evening to hug you,
the steady flame of the hearth to warm you,
the sigh of the breeze to stroke your hair,
starlight to brush your gaze,
the new rays of dawn to colour your world,
the first snowflakes of winter to line your path,
each one another wish.

I cannot bottle my love to preserve it
nor hide it in plain sight
nor extend it into the everyday
nor hold it forever
(much as I would want to).

It is there, but not there,
leaves no trace to the eye,
but is everywhere I turn;
its rhythm is constancy,
the steady pulse of the sweep of tides
over rocks, sand and stones;
it is always with me,
but I feel no weight,
and yet it is permanent.

I cannot box it for you
nor wrap it up,
tie ribbons around it
nor thread it among the flowers;
instead, each day, I place
its smallest token
at your feet
before you waken from your dreams
— whatever they may be —
and wish all of these things
for you
forever.

Aftermath

The days are as one.
They blink on and off;
the world apparently continues.

I am the centre of a stillness,
its silence born from the void
created by that vandal, Death,
as he trampled his way through our lives,
reaping his crop of darkness.

I make no noise,
am paralysed
in the midst of nothingness,
watching a soundless wake
spreading towards many lives,
skittling them all.

Echoes

From all the pieces of you
that remain
trapped on film, in photos, in sound,
I try to free the essence of who you were.

All these echoes of your soul
surround me in the air.
I grab at them, in a loop,
trying to keep you here,
but my reach is short
and you soar away from me.

Still, I snatch and grasp
with all my might,
persistently,
even as it becomes night
and the cold freezes my hands.

Cumulus

It is a day of blue and white.
I see the sky
but I do not absorb it.
Does it absorb me?
I watch a cloud
process its way to somewhere else
and then another one
and another one.
Soon the blue will turn to black
and I'll still be watching,
waiting for something
that will never arrive.

Room temperature

Room temperature is comfortable
but this room is airless,
stuffy, gently oppressive,
a benign dictator of an atmosphere.
The quietest room
in an old, large house;
noiseless, soundless, formless
and you both lie still in its centre,
the eye of this tornado of silence.

You are not you,
not the you that you were,
that you is elsewhere
and finished with this world's waking struggle,
its roiling fight until the end
— and everything is kept at room temperature.

I kiss your lips
but they are cold.
I stroke your hair
one final time,
gently, slowly, deliberately,
with all the love I have left
channelled to my fingertips,
as though this power
could somehow spark you awake.

I should forego the rest of my time
for ten minutes more.

I hold your stiff, chilled hand
in mine again,
one last touch,
and then I leave you both
forever
at room temperature.

Ruin

The front room is empty —
you can see that
from the pavement.

Nothing moves inside
from day to day.
The blinds do not alter
their position
from one night
to the next.

There is no light,
no warmth —
and slowly,
the interior cools,
frozen
on a late summer morning,
with much to be done
that day.

Now it is late autumn:
stour has settled,
cobwebs have been spun,
the warmth has left the year.

These items of our lives
decay in silence.
Only summer's ghosts
and hope's echoes
linger.
They, too, will go.

As will I,
as I must.
I leave behind my dreams
in dust.

Prelude

The sky darkens,
wraps the hills
in its winter shroud.

They are disappeared one by one
behind the curtain
that sweeps down hell's glen
from the north.

They will reappear
in full winter plumage
and I will still be chasing autumn,
trying to dam time's river
like a temporal King Canute.

Strange present

The gift I wish for this year
more than any other
cannot be bought
and will not appear.

For many, it never exists —
the few who recognise it.

Peel aside the petals
of a dozen Christmas cacti
and you will find a nothing.

But I want nothing
and I want for nothing,
yet am bombarded
by those things I do not need.

This wondrous object that I seek
this passion, this strange desire,
this tiny flame I try to keep
aglow, that it might rage to fire
eludes us all, is brief and fleeting
and when found, soon vanishes again,
yet still I search for its true meaning.

I may catch it for a day, but then
the world's distractions begin repeating,
and the noise continues till such time when
silence stalls, bows, states its intent in intervening:

"Peace on earth, goodwill to all men."

And then…
and then…
All men.
A' men.

Amen.

Solstice

The chill air cloaks this day,
brings a pause in worldly affairs,
the shortest light remains of grey,
the earth sleeps, renews, repairs.

The year halts, frozen still,
tepid sunbeams are lost in mist
while moonlight keeps its cold vigil
and frosted grass is kissed.

Scant life hides underground,
as the year's wheel turns in silence,
yet hope's gleaming fleck will be found,
flickering defiance.

The vital spark prevails
in surroundings however stark,
the catalyst that will not fail:
a first step out of the dark.

A late spring

Growth is brown and stunted,
if it is there at all;
my progress is impeded
by the cocoon wrapped around me,
protecting me from the future
but stopping me moving into it.

It will not work,
for I saw the world unseen,
the place of chaos,
drizzled with confusion,
its players skiting along its skin,
must keep busy, always busy,
the membrane of activity repelling them all.

I must have tasted sour to life
as it spat me out;
a random glitch that punctured its surface,
the ghost who accidentally lived.

Where I landed was no man's land,
where nothing was or is or could be,
but I gazed around me anyway
and behind the veil I saw
there was no one there,
holding the grand design for life.

Yet I shall know sunshine
when I feel it once more
and my joints unfurl their frozen selves,
in this blank and empty future-life,
where my nothing moves with more intent
than all the shadows cast
by the countless stars I observe
each night through deadened eyes.

Parallax child

You were a tiny speck,
you are everyone who has ever been,
you are everyone you ever knew,
you are starlight,
you are everywhere and anywhere,
nowhere and somewhere.
You are stardust,
a mote in the Great Universe,
and you are it
and it is you,
minute and enormous,
and all at once,
too much for us to comprehend,
the we who are here,
the you who never were,
because you were already everywhere
you needed to be.

Grief advisory

Everything heals in time, they say,
but not everything does.

You'll be left with a scar, they warn,
as though you could forget anyway.

Time, it takes time, they tell you,
but you find time isn't linear.

You'll remember the good times, they coax,
as though memory makes choices.

The boy is relying on you, they remind you (helpfully),
as you are crumbling inside and barely there yourself.

You've got to stay strong, keep going, they encourage,
as though the pit of weakness can be avoided.

It will get better, it will pass, they promise,
but there are days, the many days, when you want it to stay.

You'll never forget them, they remind you,

as though they weren't with you every moment of every day.

You must keep going, they implore,

and you do, of course you do, but you wonder why.

Settling

A melancholy has alighted on me lately,
a fine crust of too much life
that I cannot sweep away.

The thin film of permanence coats
this day, this hour, this minute,
settles as a concrete skim.

I try to rub it off
but it begins to set and hold firm,
impervious to my furies,
unflinching faced with stoicism,
unyielding to the rain.

I keep moving to prevent it hardening
lest it forms a cast of the husk of me;
keep moving, always moving,
an anthromachine of perpetual motion.

But sometime soon,
I'll need to pause,
look around,
survey the world again,

breathe all its airs anew
and remember every day I see
through these eyes, with this face,
each sky of slate or gin-clear blue
and all the mighty dreams I chase
are only here because of you.

Purpose

Left here
I remain
to explore
the space between
the two great silences.

In the darkest moments
I glimpsed him,
silhouetted in his uniform:
the netherworld's ambassador,
his calling card a howl,
the one that is the final lure.

Yet this time it was only noise,
but I know he shall return
and that I'll think I'll be ready
for his raven robes
and the siren music
of his pipes,
ready for the seduction
of his diplomatic charm.

For now, this is the branch
to which I cling
in the deep water
which is blackened
and already cold.

Whatever love is

A man who would be king once said,
'whatever love is'
(I paraphrase, of course),
as though he had been asked to define the impossible
and had given up.

His fieldwork would have shown him this:

the atoms of diamonds survey their own
pitiful structure compared to love;
it reaches beyond the last moon of the furthest star
in that part of the universe you cannot yet see
  - that's whatever love is.

It is more stoic than a pondering of ancient Greek
philosophers,
would catch a dozen neutrinos before breakfast,
whilst in the midst of colliding a god particle or two,
could put a smile on the Mona Lisa's face
and make Da Vinci look like a doodler
  - that's whatever love is.

It would best Cupid in an archery tournament,
outlast those pop-up items: kindness, truth and patience;
it is the something that salves the nothingness,
the balm for all those single moments wasted
-    that's whatever love is.

A movement in a symphony is white noise set next to love;
it is the sustenance of the hidden soul
you didn't know you had
-    that's whatever love is.

It is in the far and near,
in the now and then
and the still-to-be
-    that's whatever love is.

And in a meadow
gilded by prismatic summer,
where you see only the flowers,
two lovers walk together in eternity.

That's whatever love is.

Well

Nobody knows how I feel,
the depth of the well
at the centre of myself
and everything being built around it,
this hollow core.

Shout into it,
there will be no echo,
peer down it,
no light escapes
a black hole of a soul.

It is a nothing,
the nothing,
that no one else sees
nor hears nor feels,
but it is there
waiting, every day,
to swallow up
my simple wishes;
it drowns them
in the silence
of its cold, dark water.

Its only purpose: to halt and hold
— it's a Checkpoint Charlie for my spirit.

Each day,
I dive down further
into its blackness,
trying to find the bottom
so I might at least
stand upright, be still
before I have to swim once more,
rise and fight for cool, sweet air.

Temporary road closure

I'm waiting for a poem
but I have no words left in me.
Rhyme has left me
and scansion has flitted, too.

Perhaps I've nothing left to say
or my brain is tongue-tied, out of shape?

Still, I'm trying to write a poem
to express myself deliberately,
be honest, be clever
as though prose would not do,
that service station Christmas gift of language,
a bare thought and a bad one at that.

I turn the telescope in my birling head around,
observing countless brilliant points of light,
the evanescence of a billion suns,
a fountainhead of shooting stars,
the rainbow ribbons of the Merry Dancers,
criss-crossing them all.

This shows me I already told you
what I'm trying to write now,
how I'm trying to be:
'live now and be present'
— but I always think I can do better;
perhaps that's why I'm always restless
and maybe that is why I'm stuck.

For now, I shall keep on writing
and for now, I shall also stop.

Notes from a toddler

What did you do at nursery today?

I saw…
swings!
I saw…
Harry!
I saw…
garden!
I saw…
blue car!
I saw…
piano!
I saw…
park!

Everything is seen,
absorbed and processed,
food is fuel,
sleep a recharge.

The world,

a place to tear around,

break and fix

a dozen times an hour,

then repeat it all again

magical tomorrow —

a concept like today

but with strange new realms

to be explored

by tiny pioneers,

unearthing hidden hoards,

those treasure troves

of discovery,

waiting patiently

to be released

back into the light.

Two small shoes

Two small shoes,
owner gone away,
sit, as they were left,
underneath an antique wardrobe,
gathering balls of fluff and dust.

They wait with patience
for their mistress
to return home,
to take them walking
or maybe dancing
like she used to.

They wait in vain,
their only companion:
silence.

Their vigil
for the past
collides into now
and its quiet remains.

Those two small shoes
rendered mute and still.
Two small shoes
that I can never hope to fill.

For Yeeon and Steven on their Wedding Day, the day on which I was a stand-in bridesmaid.

Grand designs

I would build you a rocketship
so I could scatter petals
through the stars for you.

I would build a cloudbusting device
so it would never rain on you
and you would never be soaked
by those buses that zoom through big puddles.

I would sew together all my clothes
(well, the ones I'll not be needing)
to make the world's biggest blanket,
to keep you warm on frosty nights.

I would make a robot
out of bits and pieces from the shed
(that I shall have);
it would make you breakfast in bed
— or at least a cup of tea —
whenever I was not there.

I would learn to fence
so I could slice a way through
the freezing fog for you
when you are walking home
after working long hours.

I would hold your hand
while you sleep a thousand dreams
and stroke your hair
to hear you murmur,
and replenish your contentment.

But most of all
I shall learn from you,
kindness, patience, truth and love,
those gifts you leave every day
that cannot be built nor made
nor stitched together,
those eternal pegs
that pin our universe
to its own firmament.

Braking

I began first to slow down
when I sat down more
than I stood up
and moved about.

Technology didn't help:
too many digital sirens,
those screens of distraction
assisting the process
of sedentariness.

I prefer to call it composting,
but for what?

A future I cannot now reach
as I'm dragged further along
the path from the wrong side
of that fork in the road,
created from that one weekend last summer,
with its time-bending vigil
punctuated by a double quietus,
when many worlds collapsed at once
into an empty singularity.

A handbasket of nothing

Where are you?
Where are you both now?

I should like to know
I should like to know where you have gone

that I might follow
that I might follow you one day

each day passes
each day passes slowly in a haze of aching

each night dwindles
each night dwindles to perpetual daybreak

with its eerie grey
with its eerie grey cape of half-light

illuminating nothing
illuminating nothing recognisable

a sea estuary in midsummer
in a year of drought

and only plenty
and only plentiful zero forthcoming.

I carry myself
I carry myself in a handbasket of nothing

born from the womb
born from the womb of Hell's waiting room

and it is stuck fast
it is stuck fast in the days' quagmire

alongside the others
alongside the others who have stopped moving

I flick the vees and start crawling.

Three empty trimesters

It has been over nine months now,
as though time means anything
in a pregnancy of grief.

The bow wave still roils souls,
its long wash spills outwards:
new babies conceived will soon be born,
jobs are changed,
marriages are made,
whole new ways of living tested.

Your power to affect lives in death
is magnified by the time elapsed
since you left us all behind,
shell-shocked and wondering
what the conundrum
of the future without you
was meant to teach us.

City graveyard on a summer's day

What am I doing,

visiting a memory?

I can do that anywhere

— if I don't bury my wits

and forget to dig them up —

but once a month or thereabouts,

I choose to do it here,

in this dark oasis,

a steady glade of peacefulness

where everything is stilled today

and for all time,

but for the secret chorus of the dead

which fades in via a thousand rustles in the breeze

and the strumming of various flying insects,

picking their way through

yards and yards of cut flowers,

occasionally feasting on the fresh blooms.

Colours lie as camouflage

for many solitary tears,

a false rain that falls in silence

in the sunshine

as nature's strange cortege

traverses the hours,

a bizarre compulsion

for which no lights come up

as it blends itself

into the muted greys and greens and browns

and exits without an encore.

Time capsule

After everything happened,
I unpacked my office backpack,
my back's omnipresent shell,
and put its contents
in a large bin bag
for a span of many timeless months.

One day, it was time to excavate it
and I began to unpick
this package from another life.

There was a laptop computer,
my mobile office,
jet black and silent,
a slab of ex-IT;
a large blue notebook
full of ideas and names and numbers
from my narrowband life
in that limited corporate highway;
three ties, two sensible (even borderline trendy),
the other, the lucky one
of dancing frogs,
deployed before key meetings —

I burned that one.

Swimming goggles
for my plodding, metronomic lengths
three times a week (minimum);
a small ipod silently hiding the tunes
to which I was writing my first book;
a spaghetti of leads and chargers and pens
plus its confetti of bits of stationery;
the compact brolly,
made in China,
useless in Scotland,
when there's proper weather;
the free bag of toiletries from the Sleeper,
augmented and customised,
so I could still look presentable
if stranded for an extra evening
in Inverness or Belfast
or that faraway London place;
and always the short book of poems
by the master,
to keep me grounded, centred,
in strange psychogeographies.

But nowhere was there one

of the small notes

you used to hide in my lunchbox

or in a pocket of my rucksack

on random days to cheer me up,

nowhere in the mobile office/stereo/disco/bathroom/pool/library

that I'd convinced myself

was a second skin

was there a trace of you

and that sniper, hindsight,

let me look through its sights

and I saw back through the looking glass

to the ending of one universe

that somehow birthed this new one

where you are not here,

and saw the indelible echoes

and permanent fragments of you

that circle me constantly,

those minute satellites,

indicative of life

in closer proximity,

each one a tiny orbiting jewel

I guard jealously in my treasure box of memory.

Signs

Every day I see them:
No parking
Do not enter
Kill your speed
Caution: filling may be hot

Utilitarian placebos all.
Not once did I stumble upon
This is how to live your life
nor have a succinct
Purpose of the Universe
thrust into my path.

And as for
A Guide to Love,
even a cryptographer
would struggle with that one
(though it should be placed
within an unbroken circle,
which occasionally turns red).

No, the signs I see everywhere
are leaden neverprose,
deadening cities,
infiltrating the countryside,
their digital writers
only following orders.

Not many of them useful,
telling me what I already know
but choose to forget,
lest my simian brain
dwell on such impermanence
and overshoot its metaphysical turn-off.

First and last request

If I am part of the Universe
or it is part of me,
can I be a small, bright nodule
with light enough to see?

Can I scatter myself all through it
like dust upon the air,
so a thin film of me exists
in places everywhere?

Can I breathe it in completely
so it fills up both my lungs,
then exhale it out at speed
and stay forever young?

Can I straddle all of time
to see moments from the past,
then plough on through the present
to a future that will last?

Will I one day leave it
or live on where I please,
in a form that's somewhat altered
with a gait that mimes the breeze?

Or am I in it, of it, with it,
is it of me, my cells and soul,
this oneness of existence,
the being as a whole?

A single purpose given,
a simple plan explained:
I am it and it is me,
a brain on brane on branes.

Epicentre

Something has happened,
 — you are aware of that;
something ruptured and crushed
the atmosphere around you.
A symphony mute
under a score of muffled weeping,
tears and faces in sleeves —
but mostly it is noiseless,
a shock vacuum,
emptier than all space
but for an ink blot blackness
spreading from its centre
absorbing all around it,
levelling the interconnected world,
throttling your spirit.
You await the CPR
for your flatlining soul.

Second life

Thrown into a different timestream:
one that looked so similar,
but with hidden omissions,
scattered landmines awaiting missteps —
criss-crossed by invisible threads
that only time untangles
and fate makes me trip over daily.

These traps I try to navigate
whilst always stumbling blindly forward
— what other way can I go?

Somedays, I simply stop and watch for silence
as though it may bring a higher peace
(on some level);
I'd take that however it came packaged,
but stay too long and I start to sink
into the quicksand of memory,
its steady suction pulling me downwards
and backwards, always backwards
to the second shadow
cast by my other self,
the one who thought he knew

with such certainty
how the future would be written,
the surety revealed as fate's Ponzi scheme,
a confidence trick played out
on all the other sleepwalkers.

I fell from one place
into perpetual interregnum,
a gin trap where I scrabble wildly to locate
the hidden palace
where a new King sits,
he who may grant a freedom
or a simple pardon to breathe again,
or hand back those three wishes
I once squandered on such folderols
as I thought to be of import,
concomitant with that other life,
torn away and barrelling wildly,
so distantly, through all of time and space,
that vacuum of no discernible measure,
comprised of nowhere, nothing, naught.

But that future buried in my cells' DNA

now rests too far from here

to glimpse, to reach, to hear

or ever to be touched and caught,

even if somehow I could see it,

wish for it or breathe it,

or that gadfly King reprieve it.

Space as shadow

I stroll about this spring day,
watching the trees spill nature's confetti
as it carpets gardens and pavements,
and festoons the village with pastel polka dots.

I am remembering another day,
one that is far from here and now,
and imagining how much I would give away
to walk with you once more,

to see your curls bob gently on the breeze,
feel the grip of your small hand
as we watch a mistle thrush
survey its kingdom
from its throne atop a telephone pole

or a hen pheasant skittishly poking
through the long grass,
a dowdy nervous tic of feathers,
tremulously wondering if any of it is safe,
avoiding the invisible booby traps
set for her alone amongst the stalks and stems.

We thought we were safe,
secure as we could be in that other place
on that other day,

but now, today, I walk alone
the space next to me filled
only with a portable silence,
a vacuum as an image of you
who are not here.

So many days will be as this one,
so many days are yet to be,
the many days you'll never see.

And everywhere I go
it walks with me,
the memory of you on a day
such as this one.

Some moments, I forget,
but the space next to me
pauses and waits for me
to catch up with it
and remember once again

or I turn to you to say something
and find myself talking to a wall
(it never answers).

Nothing can exist in a vacuum
— I know that —
so where are my memories of you
or the words I would say to you?

I write them here
so they might still exist
as whispers on a page,

and still I keep on walking,
moving onwards, ever onwards,
into the temporary future,
towards the unknowable destination,
forever with that space between me
and you, on the other side of time.

Two pebbles

I lost the first pebble,
the other is kept closer still.

Our last day at the beach,
together as a family,
frittering our time,
all our forever, all our tomorrows,
with the future's cornice
already dangling above us,
casting its pall over
all our tomorrows, all our forever.

In the midst of this unseen tsunami,
you found two small white pebbles,
smooth and pure and whole.

We took them home as a minding
of that ordinary day,
even though we had gathered dozens
of these found objects.

Now, I carry the remaining one with me
everywhere I go in this other netherlife,

my permanent reminder of you,
a fleck of your measured stillness
on that quiet, normal, peaceful day.

One ordinary day amongst so many others,
but a hidden eve,
camouflaging carnage,
unremarkable at first;
now, gazing backwards from wherever I am
and striving to remember,
it looks a centred place,
the well in the midst of the oasis
from which to draw
drips and drops of solace;
the steady beat of a time misplaced
now felt each time I cradle
that small, perfect stone
between my still ageing fingers
and try to fashion a hold
on a speck of eternity.

Girl

You were never truly here
but you were real to me.
As real as my breath,
bonnie as your stillness let you be.

In your sweet face,
with its tiny, permanent features,
I saw myself
and your mother, too.

You had her ebony hair
and button nose
which she disliked
but which I loved.

And you were real,
you were real to me.

I held you
wrapped your perfect wee fingers
around one of my own,
pretended to myself

that you needed a wee heat,
willed you to move
as though sheer force of thought
and love
could animate your small, scrunched up face,

and you were real, my love,
you were real to me.

But there you stayed,
perfect in your stillness,
silent in your sleep,
not once disturbing this strange new world
with a single cry.

Yet you were real, my wee lass,
and forever will you be.

Strawsong

The year cools:
its treasure trove
in tattered clothes
falls to earth
as autumn's gold.

The light fades:
nature's dimmer switch is turned on,
the winds blow summer away,
leaves scatter and swirl,
cobwebs are disrupted,
branches graffiti shaggy, discoloured lawns.

It is dark by dinnertime,
by then and earlier still;
we hold the line
until we retreat indoors,
inside ourselves.

Drowsy flowers nod
in upright breezes,
have fits in gales,
and our music
is awakened to stave off winter's sleep,
those sweeter sounds
which glory in the gloaming.

But the notes turn dissonant,
and cascade in a whirl
and spin and tumble
in inner space
too tight for them.

They made their song of straw in summer,
a passing calligraphy
to decorate the days,
but grown spindled by December,
with broken strands
stained by mildew,
to be played once more
for memory's sake.

We lift our heads up,

sense the familiar,

give a nod to its final grace;

our eyes fill

with sparkling recognition

of another time,

a different place,

a last echo of a final line,

one more to etch onto

this weathered face.

A life in two parts

They say he has a son,
that he almost had a daughter once, too,
that his wife died young, too young;
that she saved his life,
and though he was near broken,
there was enough left.

I expected a beginning, middle and end,
but no one explained
that each segment
could be of variable length —
or perhaps they did
and I wasn't listening.

Instead, there was this:
two parts. The part that ended (too soon)
and the part that began again (immediately).

It was never like this in the movies
 — no one would believe in such a film —
and living on in the midst of it,
I kept expecting to wake up
whilst the two of you slept on.

They talked about the grieving process,

about time as the great healer,

but forgot to mention

that grief is a shapeshifter,

an expert ambusher

who never truly fades.

I remember I forgot to eat

for quite a while.

It did me no harm,

but I wouldn't recommend it as a diet.

They say that it changed him inside

and he was never the same again afterwards.

They got the last bit right:

the old self never returned,

but the new version,

forged in fire,

became unbreakable

and persisted like the frost

that lingers in the shadows

of the silent trees and stilled plants

on that type of crisp, bright February day

that fends off spring,

but loses daily

to the longer, ever stronger light.

Things you should know

You should know that the dance goes on,

that even when I am not immediately thinking about you, I still miss you,

that I miss you both,

that our wee boy is well,

that we speak about you often,

that he knows who you were,

that you loved him so much you thought that you would burst,

that you were a doctor and a fine one at that,

that you saved his daddy's life,

that you were the most honest person his daddy ever met,

that we were happy,

that you looked after him,

that you taught him how to dance and sing,

that you and Papa took him swimming,

that you were with him when daddy was at work doing 'important things';

that — far too late — I finally gained perspective, perhaps even a smir of wisdom,

that I keep going, but I wonder why,

that we all miss you so much and in so many different ways,

that there have been three babies and two marriages (so far) because you left us so early,

that we are doing good work in your name,

that you made us all become doctors,

that we tell your story to help others,

that we do this to try and save more lives,

that we hope we do you justice,

that our wee girl was beautiful and that you held her,

that our wee boy is a happy wee soul,

that I will always love you,

that you were an old soul, who was wise and kind,

and that there is a space next to me

that travels by my side everywhere I go

and it can never, ever be filled.

Inside Blazes

First questions

You ask questions,
'Where is mummy?'
How, *where* do I begin?
That she saved me but I couldn't save her?
That you had a sister?
That this carnage has destroyed me?
That you are all I have left?
What a burden to place on an unknowing child.

Within the dead zone

Stop. Just stop.
I halt my mind. Stone dead.
It wills me to traverse
these many roads to hell:
"What if..?"
"If only…"
"The future…"
"What future..?"
"But how..?"
"But why..?"

I stop it all by unleashing life:

this is it and it is now — and that is all.

Everything else is gone;

it is locked away forever,

so toxic has it become.

I sealed it in spiritual concrete

for a thousand years.

After me. After everyone.

Fingernails in a cranny

The mantra — over and over:

This. Makes. No. Sense.

I am too small to understand it,

too insignificant to change it,

but still here.

For what?

You, my best boy, obviously.

For what else?

To be defined, decoded, deciphered

and deconstructed over time.

For now, it is minute by minute,

then, a stretch to an hour.

Circumstance is my gaoler

Fate dangled me by a single strand
attached to my inflamed leg
and my body's internal collapse
...*all systems shutting down*...
and watched me wrestle and writhe,
being struck by blow after blow after blow,
stared as my being was reduced to its core,
kept vigil as my core was eviscerated
to the dust of nothing,
then released me to fall the final step.

Clarity

There is nothing now.
It is simple.
It is all erased.
Everything and all of it.
I opened my eyes and crawled out of the dirt.
The future is binary:
you and me, boy.
Two pathways.
I look at you:
innocent, bright, cheerful, alive,
and I choose the hardest route,

of spikes and rocks and stony ground,

with regulations and meaningless blandishments

strewn across its every square foot

and I fall forwards into it,

surrendering myself

to the universe once again,

trusting it to know what it is doing

— and to have my back —

as I stumble and hack at our future,

the immediate now,

the possible now,

the long now

— but the immediate now is first.

Dreamstate codicil

At your first chance to visit,

you left me these words:

'you are at the edge of the power of living with things.'

So, I had my instructions

and broke through that thin crust to the new

and began walking through Chaos' torrents,

striding to the centre of it all,

moving — always moving —

to where, one day, you both will be.

A temporarily fixed point in time

Wherever there are endless hours of darkness
and the dawn becomes the day's false summit,
remember the light cannot be lost forever,
for the sun always rises.

Whenever all you know has frozen over
and only a phantom warmth remains,
permafrost may blanket your every moment,
yet the sun always rises.

However the fates have corralled your dreams
or loaded the deck and the gun as well,
while life's shadows may look perpetual,
still the sun always rises.

Whoever is lost or has departed
leaving that never-ending ache in their stead,
the one that excavates you till you're empty,
know the sun always rises.

Whatever has befallen those around you,
devoured your time and all you have to give,
rendered all you hold exhausted,
turned the world into a place of shade,
you must cross the scattered debris
and carry on so as to live,
for each day resets at midnight clear
and the sun always rises.

The years, they fly

(On Hogmanay)

Some years sidle up to their end
under twin guises of darkness and distraction
and steal away to memory
before they're missed,
so tired are they of the party

(the dance goes on).

Other years are more outgoing,
will be missed when they leave;
we smile as they burst out the door
and sway off singing down the street,
their nocturnal melodies scattering the gloom
until they, too, are blended into the past
to which this night of all nights
stands lone watchman

(and the dance goes on).

Then there are the wallflowers,
the many more who need to be there
to cradle the spark
that lights up the moon,
the muted crowd we won't notice till the end
when we realise they were necessary

(still the dance goes on).

So easily are our heads distracted,
we seldom see the new year as it coughs nervously
and shuffles its feet,
conquering its nerves to enter

(yet the dance goes on).

We will puzzle over its shape, its potential, *the future,*
this Rubik's Cube of new time,
further, on into the tomorrow that's already today,
as we tune ourselves into the looming hereafter
in which our binocular gaze searches
this strange arrivals lounge
for a bottle that fizzes orange

(and ever, the dance goes on).

Praise of a woman

She was a gift,
with a soft and beautiful voice
who could mimic others' songs,
and whose own song brightened many days.

She was a gift to everyone,
her healing stopped myriad people
from falling any further;
she repaired with kindness and love.

She was a gift to the world,
one who made so many
smile and laugh their troubles clear
— she always knew the right prescription.

She was the loveliest gift
who lived honestly through her deeds,
a gift so great, that at the end,
the fates paid her forward:
a doctor for those in greatest need.

All authorial proceeds from sales of this book will be donated to FEAT - Sepsis Research (Registered Charity in Scotland: SC044017).

For more information about sepsis, please visit:
sepsisresearch.org.uk

16014105R00047

Printed in Great Britain
by Amazon